GIRL, IF I KNEW THEN WHAT I KNOW NOW

K.J. Dixon

COPYRIGHT 2021 K.J. DIXON

This work is licensed under a Creative Commons Attribution-Noncommercial-No Derivative Works 3.0 Unported License.

Attribution — You must attribute the work in the manner specified by the author or licensor (but not in any way that suggests that they endorse you or your use of the work).

Noncommercial — You may not use this work for commercial purposes.

No Derivative Works — You may not alter, transform, or build upon this work.

Print ISBN: 978-0-9980109-4-6
Digital ISBN: 978-0-9980109-5-3

For Bree, of course. And for little Kristen too. I love you both very much.

First of all, air kisses and virtual hugs to all my girlfriends, family members and the women I randomly meet in places like grocery stores and hair salons. I love the way we can instantly connect over a shared experience. We start off trying to help each other by asking for a quick opinion on a brand of peanut butter or complimenting a sister with a cute hairstyle and several minutes later are bonding and giggling while saying, "girrrrl!"

Fortunately for me, most of us don't ever mind sharing the good lessons we've learned in life as well as the bad advice we've received (and sometimes suffered). Most of us will agree that there's some advice you keep, some to which you come back, and some you just use to give you a good occasional laugh. This book is full of conventional wisdom, sage advice and bad advice too. It reminds us of the lectures we've all heard from our mamas, aunties and grannies and even gives us a few we wish we'd had.

I suggest you grab your favorite bottle of wine (or sparkling water?), a big glass and a comfortable seat. Pour liberally from your bottle and find your reflection in a mirror (or depending on how much you've poured, maybe your beverage) before you start sipping. Smile at yourself. Regardless of whatever the person staring back at you looks like at the moment, release the urge to judge yourself. Then think about what a miracle it is that you have survived as much shit as you have in your life so far and celebrate that for a second. Know that you are exactly where you are supposed to be right now. It's true.

There is no reason why you must read this book of anecdotes and advice in the order presented. Find a section that speaks to whatever you're struggling with presently, marinate on it, and laugh a little. Know that once you shut it close (and even before you opened it), you are fully prepared to handle whatever life throws at you. There is no handbook for womanhood, motherhood, perfect health, friendship, wifedom or singledom, workdom or any other words that I could make up, but in its place, here is some of the best (and worst) advice I could find to share with you.

Cheers my friends, until next time.

Love, Dating & Marriage
9

Health & Self Care
17

Smart is the New Sexy
25

Career
29

Children
33

Spirituality, Religion, & Good Living
39

LOVE, DATING & MARRIAGE

The ability to really connect with other people is one of the greatest gifts God could ever give us. It's cool as hell to be able to share your story with someone, and to know that they actually get it.

-KJD

NOW, LET'S GET straight to it. They really did mean well when they told me…

- No woman should ever be broke because she is literally sitting on her own gold mine.

- What you don't tell won't hurt you. Enjoy life and be careful.

- Find a man who loves you more.

- Focus on your husband's good qualities, forget the bad as often as you can.

- Never go to bed angry.

- It's okay to take some things to the grave with you.

- Common sense isn't very common anymore.

- Get married at least once—try it. What's the worst that can happen? Divorce?

- Communication will save or sever your relationship.

- Don't be afraid to get couples' therapy.

- Continue to date.

- Be quick to forgive.

- Be honest about who you are. Be bold about what you want.

- If you give it up too fast, he'll have no reason to stick around.

And I've found most of it to be true! But what I *really* wish I'd known then was...

- You should be sure to keep the fights clean and the sex dirty.

- Be present in your sexual experiences. Learn to understand your body so that you can teach your lover what you like.

- Some men are aroused too quickly to ever actually enjoy. Move on when you learn this.

- Don't try unprotected sex until you get married. You might find that you like it and I can't get you out of trouble or pull a bug out of your ass.

- Foreplay begins long before you reach the bedroom.

- Use toys. Lots of them.

- Clench those muscles. All of them.

- Kegels are the best exercises ever invented.

- Surprise him often with favors.

- Marriage is hard, yet rewarding. Be willing to give and compromise.

- God has to be the ever-present third person in your marriage.

- There will be times when you can hardly stand him. Sometimes many of them.

- Love is an action word. Love is an active choice.

- Identify his love languages.

- Teach him yours.

- Lick on him like he's your favorite flavor ice cream cone.

- Never settle.

- Even good sex can't fix a raggedy man.

- Find someone who stimulates you mentally. Even the best sex gets old when y'all get old.

- Anal sex isn't for everybody. But perhaps you should try it.

- Settle into marriage when you're ready. You don't go to college for an M-R-S degree.

- Have a relationship that makes you happy—not everyone else.

- There is absolutely nothing wrong with loving sex.

- You sometimes need to just keep a good water-based lubricant in your nightstand drawer.

- All cowgirls should learn how to ride a horse backwards.

Relationships and marriages are small businesses that should be mutually beneficial. Most of the time, people just want to feel understood and loved. *When you're with the right person*, you'll naturally improve one other. Loving your partner won't feel like a chore. Each of you will get exactly what you need, yet the relationship won't feel transactional.

But check this out. Happiness, even within our romantic relationships, is a state of mind that you can choose to enter and exit all by yourself. Experience teaches us that if you don't know and love yourself, you can rotate partners but still manage to keep the same problems (for example, if you think yourself fit to be the wife of an alcoholic you may find yourself frequently attracted to men who drink too much. The first might be named Tim, the second Tom and the third Ted, but all three will abuse it). Sometimes we're programmed to attract destructive behavior by the people who raised us (I call this hard wiring). At other times we program ourselves based on a dysfunctional relationship or experience (though I hear that this particular type of malfunction is easier to correct, and I like to refer to it as soft wiring). Either way, you have to be self-aware and willing to do the hard work of re-programming, re-parenting and re-wiring your own-damn-self if you want to improve your outcomes. None of us are exempt from these fundamental principles. Broken pieces tend to attract each other like shards of glass. And like those sharp pieces, they often end up cutting each other.

You can only invite real, true and deep love into your consciousness after you are made whole. If you're struggling to do this, get a therapist and Jesus on the main line.

HEALTH & SELF CARE

If you have a problem with me, call me. If you don't have my number to call me, you don't know me well enough to have a problem with me.
-Unknown

THEY REALLY DID mean well when they told me (please, and I mean PLEASE don't try this at home)…

- Give yourself a vinegar douche after sex and you won't get pregnant.

- Black people don't need therapists.

- Let him cheat honey, he'll be back. He knows where home is.

- You might as well stay with him since you had his baby.

- You don't have to like his family—you're marrying him, not them.

- Nothing. (Insert your own cricket sounds here. No advice has been my worst advice. The women who come before you can hold the keys to your success and be the salve for your wounds.)

- Flour water will lower your blood pressure.

- Ain't nothing wrong with your ass.

- Don't let anyone jump (leap) over you because your stomach won't grow (you won't be able to get pregnant).

- Prenatal yoga and acupuncture are not for black women.

- Eat for two! You're having a baby.

- Put butter on your burns.

- If you eat sugar you will catch "the sugar."

- Douching is good for you.

- Any attention is good attention.

I was raised in the Deep South at a time when treating people with respect wasn't a suggestion—it was a requirement. My parents—both from Florida and only a generation or two removed from slavery, then later, sharecropping—taught me very early in life that adding the tiny words "ma'am" or "sir" to any statement could not only demonstrate respect, but could also potentially save my life. By putting a little bit of added respect on my declarations I might accomplish anything—like perhaps persuade a teacher to allow me to take a much needed bathroom break from class, or in instances of danger more grave than a pee break, allow me to avoid unnecessary conflict with the self-righteous, intolerant adult bigots who sometimes wondered how an awkward brown girl like me could walk around this world with such confidence. My "ma'am" or "sir" validated some folks in ways I still can't understand. But for most, it was simply an acknowledgement of my common respect and general appreciation for all of God's people.

As I began to grow into an adult, I continued my efforts to give due regard to the feelings, wishes and rights of others—regardless of their circumstances. As a staff nurse in the hospital where I worked, I'd show the cleaning staff the same amount of professional appreciation as the Chief Executive or Nursing or Financial Officer. And unless someone had offended me terribly, I had genuine, good intentions for the well-being of all others.

If the years of my life that preceded motherhood taught me to be considerate of others, the years after ushered me toward a state of total selflessness. After marrying and becoming a mother, I instinctively learned to eat, sleep, dress, pray for, care for and live after anyone who depended on me to make it through his or her day. On many a days I realized that I had forgotten to feed myself dinner the night before, or bathe my own ass the morning of, because I was so engrossed in the tasks that accompanied caring for someone else.

And then one day something happened. I became ever-so-slightly resentful of anyone who received my respect, my attention, my love, more than the woman inside me! Work. Dish-washing. Vacuuming. Sex. Problem solving. Budgeting. Meal planning. Grocery shopping. Cooking. Listening. Explaining. Teaching. On cue? Or on command? For that silent, neglected woman, and only she alone, had bargained and partnered with God to sustain me as I frivolously dispensed my resources to the world. It seemed that she who had earned the right to receive my utmost respect (me!), received only the leftovers and least of it. I vowed, on that day, to add myself to the long list of folks who required my respect and who had earned my love.

There is a long, hilarious tale that would explain exactly how and when that happened. But that is another story for another day.

Since that time I've spent my first waking five minutes each morning asking myself what I need. More sleep? Mouthwash? A mimosa? A new replacement for an old satin scarf? No problem ma'am, I'll get that right away for you! Respect, an outward extension of love, is due to myself before I can pay it to anyone else. And while I'm always considerate of others, respectful to the general population and loving to my loved ones, I give the lady who lives inside me the most deferential treatment by far.

Funny things happen when you love yourself properly. The folks around you suddenly feel even more of your sunshine, and everyone is better because of it.

I don't give a damn what the self-proclaimed relationship experts on the internet tell you. Love yourself and respect everyone around you. That is the only way everyone wins.

So to get back to the subject, what I really wish I'd known then was…

- Not to wait so long to start seeing a therapist. Most healthy people seek one and keep one.

- Taking care of your health is the truest form of self-love. Demonstrate love to your insides by taking care of them.

- Don't trust the labels on junk food.

- Get sleep.

- Get rest. It's not the same thing.

- Let go of fast food early. Don't wait until you're 40.

- Take care of your mental health.

- Go for walks in the park because nature will teach you a lot about life.

- No is a complete sentence. And no explanation has to follow it.

SMART IS THE NEW SEXY

I AM A nerd and damn proud of it. At a time when most girls my age were starting to like boys, I was starting to like science. Interestingly, today's celebrities include graduates of my former schools' advanced math and science programs who went on to become scientists and save the world. Did it really have to take COVID to make y'all like girls with glasses? Damn.

Anyway, I also wish I'd known…

- To eat healthy as often as possible.

- Not everything good is good for you.

- Get your boobies checked often and prioritize your pap smears!

- Healthy eating starts in your childhood.

- Listen to your body. Pay attention to every ache. They all mean *something*.

- Go to the dentist every six months.

- Floss at least once per day to protect your teeth.

- Exercise regularly.

- You can't ever eat too many fresh fruits and vegetables. A little olive oil, salt and garlic can make almost anything taste better.

Your spiritual health, physical health and mental health are interconnected. This is science! Don't believe me? Grieve the loss of a loved one and then tell me that you don't feel pain in your chest. Or for a less morbid example, entertain the company of someone who you don't trust and then convince me that your stomach doesn't hurt. If your heart aches, chances are your body will too.

As fancy and as lovely as modern medicine is, taking care of your soul is the best way to take care of your body. Stuffing your stomach won't soothe an empty heart, but it will make you fat and eventually probably give you diabetes.

CAREER

Quit shrinking for other people. Some of us were never meant to fit in any-damn-way.

-KJD

WHAT I *REALLY* wish I'd known then was...

- Find your voice in the workplace early and always speak your truth.

- Black women are game-changers.

- A jealous sister is no more helpful to you than a stranger. Be kind and be careful. And please understand—jealousy is a compliment. Don't feel anger toward jealous people—feel gratitude. Just feel it from a distance!

- You really do have to be twice as good (and I know good and damn well you know what this means).

- Take control of your career. Show up and be your best every day. There's usually little room for error.

- Focus on your passion. Your talents will make room for you.

- Find an exit strategy from any job and keep it in your back pocket.

- Never make coffee at work or bring your pot in from home. If you start making the daily pot of coffee they will always expect you do it. Don't start something you can't finish. Don't unknowingly turn into the "help."

- Learn to work around distractions. People will sometimes plant them intentionally. Drown out the noise and see only your success.

- Take an etiquette class.

- Dress the part. You will always be judged by your appearance.

- You can't wear the same dress to church, the club and to work!

- Be assertive but slow to anger. People can't wait to throw you into that stereotype.

- Be mindful of your tone and smile often.

- Be your own boss if you want. You are capable and you are enough.

- Treat others the way you want to be treated.

- Never doubt the woman you know you are.

- Let your drive for success always be bigger than your fear of failure.

- Fuck most people's opinions.

- Allies may surprise you. God sends them in all sorts of colors, ages, shapes and from the places you'd least expect.

- Beware of crabs in your bucket.

- Limit self-disclosure in the office. You don't go to work in order to make friends.

- Sometimes you won't get the promotion you deserve. Rebound quickly. Avoid bitterness. Bloom wherever you are planted. That's when the real magic happens.

- You know what happens when you do your best? Everything. You never know who is noticing you.

CHILDREN

BREE WAS A toddler when the Tickle Me Elmo toys became the obsession of all pre-school aged children.

Oh, how I hated all those damn toy commercials that would begin airing at the onset of Christmas season (which, by the way, seemed to start earlier and earlier each year). There the two of us would be, together in her play space, watching Blue's Clues or Doc McStuffins or Dora The Explorer, learning how to find and use clues or bandage a scrape or discover jewel treasures in make-believe caves, when suddenly one hundred commercials for one hundred different toys would interrupt our regularly scheduled television programing by blaring catchy songs and bright colors and somehow expertly convince my baby that she needed some new shit.

"Mama?" she'd call out to me in her very articulate-though-tiny voice before looking my way to see if I was ready to listen.

I was already looking at her. And I was always listening.

"I like Elmo," she'd say.

"And I know you do, baby," I'd tell her.

I'd spend the next few weeks pretending that I didn't know what Santa was going to bring her.

Sometimes I'd get just as excited as Bree with Christmas anticipation.

That year I must have missed the memo that informed parents of two and three-year-olds that Elmo's ass was on back order.

I went to Target, Wal-Mart and Toys R Us at least ten times in ten days in effort to find a toy shelf with at least one Elmo on it. When I finally caught one, it was because I'd arrived at the store about an hour outside of the city before 7:00 am and waited on the truck to arrive.

Talk about being proud of myself. Super-mom for the win! How long before Christmas? Now I could hardly stand the wait!

Finally it came. But when Bree opened her beautifully-wrapped, long and hard sought Elmo toy from its box on Christmas morning, she somehow seemed less enthusiastic than I was. She smiled, but that wasn't enough. I was desperate for validation to confirm that I was the coolest mom on the planet for producing the coveted Elmo! Obviously sensing my neediness and anxiety, she scooted once on her feet, but I wanted her ass to give me a full on happy dance.

And Elmo wasn't her only Christmas toy that year. To win Bree's affection, Elmo had to compete with a portable Barbie hair salon, some Play-Doh and a pool float with a shark face.

Unbeknownst to me at that time, she didn't give a damn about any of them.

I eventually arrived at this sad, disappointing conclusion on my own. There I was, scraping Christmas leftovers off of some dishes one evening just a day or two after the holiday when my thoughts of Dawn dish soap bubbles, porcelain and macaroni and cheese were pleasantly interrupted by Bree's giggles. I'd noticed her playing with what I'd assumed to be her new toys in the living room from the corner of my eye, but when I whipped my head around to see what'd made my daughter laugh so heartily, I was shocked at what I saw. My sweet baby girl was sitting in the middle of our living room, thoroughly entertained by an empty paper towel roll made of cardboard.

Was that the same paper towel roll that I just threw on the floor after a failed attempt to score a three-point with it into the kitchen trash but missed the can by a few inches?

Couldn't possibly be.

But why yes, yes it was that paper towel roll. And she was clearly smitten by it.

I turned my attention back to my dishes, this time determined not to break anymore wine goblets (my original set of six had already been reduced to four), sure that her love affair with the paper towel roll would be short-lived and fleeting. Any minute now, Bree would pick up that expensive and elusive Tickle-Me-Elmo that I'd stalked a delivery truck man in order to have under the tree by December 25th.

Fast forward to the good part, that never happened. Within six months Elmo had been donated to our local good will.

Moral of the story. Kids don't need expensive toys. They need happy parents and simple, loving, comfortable experiences.

That is all.

I find that I sound very much like my own mama when I say…

- When your children are young they work on your nerves. As they grow up they work on your heart.

- Ignore anyone who asks you if your childbirth experience was natural.

- Just a tiny ass-whooping still goes a long way.

- Don't spoil your children to make up for what you didn't have. Nothing will ever make up for what you didn't have.

- Don't let the baby sleep with you. He or she will be eighteen years old and still in your bed.

- Don't tell yourself that your baby has allergies as an excuse to give her Benadryl. If her ass is up, she's just up.

- Pumping after breastfeeding really does encourage a healthy milk supply.

CHILDREN

- Labor pain is a million times more painful than menstrual cramps. You pay for those nine free months in the end.

- Once they are here you cannot push them back up there. It's been tried.

- Start therapy before your children become teenagers.

- Stay in touch with your inner child. Remember that you've been where they are.

- Children don't ask to be here—never make them feel as though you did them a favor by raising them.

- Children learn to speak to themselves by hearing the way you speak to them.

- People will treat your children the same way that you do. Read that again.

- Parenthood introduces you to your partner all over again.

- There is a difference between influencing, parenting, and just flat out trying to re-hardwire little people. Guide your children to become whoever they were meant to be.

- Kids give the best advice. Just ask them for it.

- You don't know what tired is until you have a baby.

But what I really wish I'd known then was…well hell, now that I think about it, everything she said turned out to be true.

SPIRITUALITY, RELIGION, & GOOD LIVING

I have never missed a friend that I've lost. I love the way God orchestrates all my plans before I can even dream them.

-KJD

- There is such a thing as reading too much.

- Let your food be your medicine, but balance means everything. Men and children like to smell bacon frying when they wake up in the morning.

- Despite how you may feel right now keep going to church. One day you'll be thankful that you did.

- Don't trust everything you see. Even salt can look like sugar.

- Keep praying baby, the Lord can change anything.

- Don't be a CME member—only going to church on Christmas, Mother's Day and Easter.

- Do not ask everyone to pray for you. You don't know who their God is or what they're praying for on your behalf.

- Faith will sustain you when nothing else can or will.

- Tithe and praise the Lord.

- God don't like ugly.

- Trust God.

- Trouble don't last always.

- You may ask God why you. God asks why not you.

- Let Him fight your battles.

- Don't forget to pay your tithes.

- Pray about everything.

- Avoid the preacher's kids.

- Ministers are easily distracted. Cross your legs at the ankle in church.

- Trust your gut—that's where the Lord speaks to you.

- Wearing red makeup or nail polish does not make you a whore.

- God loves and accepts you. He wants you to realize your highest potential.

- Going to church doesn't make you a Christian any more than going to McDonalds makes you a hamburger.

- Conduct acts of service. Be God's hand and feet.

- Take communion when offered. Repent often.

- God loves you always.

- You are exactly where you are supposed to be.

- Trust that God knows the other side of your plan. Stick to His, not your own.

- Be decent. Leave something to the imagination.

- Stay in your lane. Everybody has their own journey.

- Trust the process.

- Trust your instincts.

- There is never a testimony without a test.

- Be obedient to God's commands.

- Listen more than you speak. It's only when you are quiet that you can hear God speaking.

ACKNOWLEDGMENTS

I have written many things, and this little book has totally turned out to be one of my favorites. Michelle Fairbanks and Adam Bodendieck, I couldn't continue to make art without you. Thank you Gina, Chiquita, Nina, Adonness, Angie, Rekita, Edwina, Shekina, Erin, Ebony, Charna, and every other girlfriend or stranger who has ever acknowledged that I'm not the only woman who has ever experimented with the wisdom passed down to me over the ages from my elders just to find out that it could have used some improvement. Ruth, I love you for coaching me and keeping me sane. Love to my own mama, Carolyn, for pouring her whole heart into me my entire life. Annette, the world's greatest godmother, has held me down though everything and loves me like I'm her blood. Everybody needs an auntie like Terry and another one like Cherrie. Thank you for helping me to be great! Bryan and Bree, how do you manage to support every single thing I do? I love you I love you I love you. And last, but certainly not least, many thanks to my dear readers for letting me always be unapologetically me. I cuss a little and I still love Jesus a lot. Amen.

ABOUT THE AUTHOR

K.J. Dixon is more than a lover of the literary world. She is a self-improvement guru, gifted storyteller and motivational speaker, listening-ear to her friends, devoted wife and doting mother. She loves all things festive and fun and lives in Atlanta with her family. Learn more by visiting with her at www.thekjdixonexperience.com.

www.ingramcontent.com/pod-product-compliance
Lightning Source LLC
Chambersburg PA
CBHW070803050426
42452CB00012B/2468